Of Ink & Ashes

Sumayyah Ali

BookLeaf Publishing

India | USA | UK

Made with ❤ on the BookLeaf Publishing Platform

www.bookleafpub.in

www.bookleafpub.com

Dedication

To all those who have used Ink to discover themselves &
to rise from the Ashes, and to those whose eyes have
found poetry woven into every walking moment.

Preface

When the idea of "Of Ink and Ashes" first took shape, someone told me that I should pen it down as an experiment. To see if it would be received well. Another acquaintance told me something on similar lines, saying that if nothing else, it would be an experiment on society.

Rest assured, this is not an experiment. Neither is this simply a casual dabble.
After having given it shape, I realized that it speaks to the ways in which poetry has helped me process and navigate complex emotions whether they be related to socio-political scenarios, personal frustrations, moments of grief, or realizations drawn from research and study.

Initially, I found myself drawn to honest, unpolished words, the same language we use in everyday conversation. I discovered that in the midst of the 'little things' that make us genuinely happy and the small mishaps that cause us to 'lose it' and breakdown in front of a computer, there's an array of ideas and feelings that could be explored.
Whether it was the clumsy stumble down a flight of stairs, the unexpected pain of a bruise, or the subtle,

almost dazed moments of wonder or curiosity, practically everything I experienced, was a poem that I wanted to write.

The title, "Of Ink and Ashes," perfectly sums up this journey. The ink symbolizes that spark of creativity, the act of putting down thoughts and feelings that can last far beyond the moment in which they were written. It speaks to the concept of how thinking and learning fuel the words that we form and as a consequence, our understanding, perceptions, ideas, actions, experiences and so much more.

In contrast, ashes remind us of the fleeting nature of life, the inevitable end that follows every beginning, and the sorrow and decay that sometimes leave us feeling raw and exposed. As though we were ashes, exposed to the wind. Adding to it, the precarious nature of the multiple cultures that we are expected to live in tune with. Yet, within those ashes, there's also the hope that arises from empathy, discipline, resolve, patience and purpose, a quiet assurance that from what is lost, something new can emerge.

The modern craving for constant, sensational stimulation, I believe, is eroding our ability to recognize the marvels and dignity in the world around us, even if they were present in but a smile, and this has further concerned me. With this collection, I can only hope to contribute toward a shift nurturing a more refined sensitivity that literature can offer, counteracting the degrading trends of contemporary society.

Embracing a style that employs symbols that are easy to recognize and understand, if not relate to, I have built on the idea that the appeal of poetry, lies not in what it is literally stating, but in discerning the layers hidden under the simple verses of genuine expression.

While I acknowledge that these poems express strong emotions on various subjects, I want to make it clear that they are not intended to promote any particular ideas, incite any actions, and or advocate any specific beliefs. At their core, they are simply personal reflections and emotions captured in writing. As such, I disclaim any responsibility for any interpretations or actions arising from them.

So, as you flip through these pages, I ask you to look at it as you would any thought process- messy, unpredictable, and perhaps irrational and altering. Let 'Of Ink and Ashes' remind you of the human spirit in all its raw, unfiltered glory.

P.S. Still however, if you find that I have been incapable of articulating everything that I have so far addressed, I sincerely hope that the poems can do the explaining, for I have always been far better utilizing them anyways.

Acknowledgements

Alhamdulillah.

I cannot begin without expressing my deepest gratitude to my parents and family, whose steadfast support and impeccably timed counsel have not only kindled my curiosity, but have also kept me both sane and well-fed.

To my best friend, cousin, and unofficial editor, I do not think any amount of acknowledgement would do justice to the effort you have put in to tolerate me in all my excruciating and confused glory.

A sincere shout out to the group which began at a museum, and to my friends who call themselves 'Blood, Sweat and Tears'. Thank you for the laughs, the listening ears, and for always reminding me that even the toughest days can make you cry tears of stupid joy. I genuinely appreciate how you have helped me want to make this a reality.

To my sister although your subtle humor is better tucked away in the quiet of your mind, you always manage to pull me back to reality. I thank you equally for that unforgettable moment when your near-poetic wit almost inspired a poem.

To my professors, your lectures have always proved to be the best places for my thoughts to venture into the depths of reflection and comprehension. I am forever indebted to your guidance and imparted knowledge.

Most importantly, I must acknowledge BookLeaf publishing, whose faith in my work and the countless works of budding writers has helped turn a pile of ideas into substantial literature.

You have all undoubtedly been an integral part of bringing "Of Ink and Ashes" to life.

Of Ink and Ashes

I tell you that my head hurts
That I fell down the stairs
Not how my legs just gave up
Or how I was running out of air

I pricked myself with a needle
To get splinters out of my hand
Convinced myself it wasn't lethal
But now I'm left with a swollen band

Shall I worry you with my notions?
Can I lie about my fatigue?
No, but I'll let you dress my blisters
And help me walk across the street

I'm afraid to tell you my stomach aches
Or how I may have ruptured a vein
For you may ask me to see a doctor
Who's not qualified for my pain

I feel cursed with the capacity
To see through our races' scurry
Why, I cannot ask a friend
To unwind in a hurry

I'm bleeding in this gallery
Filled with Ink and Ashes
Reading raw stories of the past
Tracing wise men's splashes

They tell me of their time
Of institutions of ideas
Professing secrets shaping history
And or crafting the divine

I reflect on ours lamenting
Tasting bitter human lime
Blades and circuits shape our temples
Spirited souls feel undefined

I grow tired for the hearts
That die beating, unheard
Like a prisoner upon whom
False claim was incurred

Here I stare into space
To keep up with our pace
But it was lost on me how
It too, was a vacuum of a place

So I carry this listlessness
Across this burning sand
For I cannot have you fathom
This sadness in my hands.

Discerning Genocide.
A child's plea to understand

A question they ask echoes in my mind
Is it genocide? How do we define?

The systematic carnage, or the bloodshed's design?
My mothers slaughter, or my fathers virtuous crime?

You're asking a child in a land of rubble and plight
By lack of a choice, running, tired, hungry, I'll fight

""*I'm still alive*"", but in which state?
Deceased, deprived, and my brother nowhere in sight

I fled my home, to the "safe-zone"
And cursed myself for trusting leaflets thrown

I hear the screams, the tears, the cries
As I go to sleep in a tent at night

Is it the intent, the deliberate aim
To wipe out a people, to erase their name?

I cannot ask my teacher, nor raise my hand
My pencil was silenced, dreams turned to dust and sand

I asked my uncle, is it the rain?
Do not worry, he said, it is my bane

Courts, councils, conventions for what gain?
For the rights to defend or define some claims?

My grandma said, it's a pattern, a plan
All I wish to do is understand

Do we search for the rhetoric, or the hate speech
The dehumanization, or the demonization's reach?

Do we count the bodies, the lost and the slain
When their numbers do not even account for the pain

Do we measure the suffering, the anguish, the fear
The displacement, the trauma, or the years?

How do we determine, how do we know
If genocide's dark shadow looms and grows?

Is it the numbers, the scale, the scope
Or is it the intent, the heart's darkest hope?

The answer lies in the eyes of our dead
The voices of survivors, the tears they've shed
It lies in the truth, the facts, the evidence too
And the courage to call it what it is, anew.

Fractured Frameworks

When silhouettes offend sight
For sleeping oblivious at night
Who are we to reprimand or despise?
Dwelling at the bottom of a well, aren't we compromised?"

A gravity-bound existence
We cannot falsify
Deviant behavior
We cannot justify

Rape of a wife
Is socially acceptable?
Hear the death of a mother
Is maritally unacceptable

Demolition of a mosque
Was spiritually valuable
While secular policies
Are constitutionally impossible

These juxtapositions have been designed
At the cost of integrity, of equity
Frameworks fractured and flawed
Have 'evolved' through history

You see the shipment of arms
Has been easily disposable
Segregation of waste however
Is exorbitant and unviable

Colonial conquest
Was inherently exploitational
But the annexation of land
Is frugally reasonable

Freedom for slaves
Had been strategically applauded
While mass incarceration
Remains culturally systemic

Reparations denied
Have been historically neglected
Now, because It is okay for a country
To be economically dependent

Peace treaties are broken
For it is militarily expedient
War crimes are forgiven
Diplomatically convenient

Free speech is curtailed
Nationally protected
Generations of culture
Have been burnt down, cremated

With artifacts of trials
Predisposed and morally misguided
Watch how our organs are now
Museums corporately orchestrated

Through fickle bargains
And compromises made
Do we see the reflections
Of our own shame?

Have we been accomplices
In this twisted trade?
Or will we rise and forge
A new path to reclaim?

For I beg you to see that in some silences
We are complicit too
In the perpetuation of systems
That oppress and subdue.

A Refugee from Grief

Charles Bukowski said that "too often the only escape is
sleep"
A frail excuse to forget the weight that we keep.

I think once, we believed
In the beauty of the world
In the kindness of strangers
And the love that unfurled

But like a flower
That withers in the cold
Our faith has been shaken
And the hearts have grown old

Many searched for answers
In literature new and old
In physiology, psychology
Or medicine to unfold

Few turned to the stars
The whispers of the wind
Adrift in oceans of desperation
To find a place called home

We've tried to hold on to hope
To grasp it tight
But it slips through our fingers
Like sand in the night

Charles Bukowski said that "too often the only escape is
sleep"
But even in dreams, the trauma creeped

Mine or yours
The screen would scream
Awake at night
For we had witnessed an ugly scheme.

Be it Africa, Ethiopia, Ukraine, Gaza
Sudan, Syria, Congo or Columbia
In this distraught domain, we're searching for relief
A respite from the pain, a refugee from the grief

Yes, Charles Bukowski said, "Too often, the only escape is sleep."

But then I wonder, have we explored the depths of belief?

In humanity, tolerance, reason or prayer

Perhaps in its warmth, we'll learn to find *some* reprieve.

Castles of Glass

A heartstring pinches
Every time I speak to you
And every nerve flinches
Under your riposte

If not from the anticipation
They recoil
Understanding drains me
How do I define?

You speak of my faults
The repercussions of my thoughts
Yet somehow I can't *bare* to speak of yours
For I know that they may be the repercussions of yours

How browbeaten must you be
To let it out so
How tired of the time stretching out
Your patience, grace and glow

I can forgive you for explosions
And won't mind picking up the debris
But how do I explain
The shortcomings that *you* see

They aren't innately independent
Nor intent on causing harm
They are pleas for mercy
Supplications to hold your arm

How do I make you forgive me
For mistakes like sleeping in
For snapping at you or just
Running away to a homegrown inn

It doesn't feel nice I swear
I want this escapism to go away
But who am I to speak of feelings
When I see yours bleeding out in an abyss of disarray

It pains me to know that
A lot of them I may have caused
Which is why I don't want you knowing
The cause of my infringements, or anxious trots

Know them just as so
Triggers wiser left unawaken

Don't dwell deeper into my heart
Here lay thoughts better left unspoken

Label me discourteous
It'll be a lesser evil to confess
It'll be easier on your soul
To ignore this inner turmoil I can't profess

Of my precarious being
Or my frivolous loss
Emotions left behind
And secrets to torch

I'll make it my burden to bare
And cut out my tongue Alas
For I don't care if my broken shards are used
To build your *Castles of Glass*.

When The Sirens Fall Asleep

Put down your hats
Lay off your coats
Let us sit down a while
To grieve the ways of the world

The countryman resigns to the businessman's appeal
And the politician precipitates this terrific ordeal
Where are the Malalas and the Mandelas?
The Gandhis, the Lincolns, or the Luthers?

For now they take vows
But their words are a game
Here suppress the press
And there deny platforms to the educationally trained

Each pact and promise
A feather, a flame
Each action, a card shuffled
Or to be dealt in vain

Children through screens
Have their innocence sold
To profits that grow
While their future grows cold

Rivers run black
Where the factories tread
Workers are hungry
Oh, but their hands are well fed

Countless cities glitter
With hollow delight
While the homeless sleep
Under the starless sky

The affluent frame their names
Cribbing about fine wine
Build towers, firms and fame
Pouring billions into AI's design

Yet the impoverished suffer
Struggling to survive
In anguish about their ailments
Are left *crying*, asking "*why?*"

Weight of arms bear down
Worthy pacts and treaties weep
Empty chairs gather dust
As alliances fray and enemies they keep

The poets speak of peace
Crafting silence, painting drought
As power, not the truth
Draws the most crowded crowd

So we sit and we grieve
As the fires catch seas
Tell me, *where will we be*
When the sirens fall asleep?

Tidal Waves

Petals fall and hair turns gray
Power flips in the light of day

Tireless winds causing surface waves
Yet our lands are swept by tidal waves

Storms are brewed by those of might
So ocean beds bestir the tsunamis right

The polar bear, with its unipolar growl
Arousing anger, playing foul

Unchecked power like fish to land
A strike too strong may scar and brand

Global South's luck, a tale of weight
Hegemony's price, the fear of fate

Order seldom grows from one
A guiding force when calming storms has begun

Two have tried with mirrored stares
Attempts at balance plummeting to Parcae's lair

Cold winds blew where walls were raised
Bitter were the times when men were encaged

How mortar was checked, and accords sealed
In sifting sand, shells of hope revealed

Still, every dance on tightropes spun
Could end in fire, a spar begun

Groupings now built where once were none
A jungle where many lions run

Chaos lurks where paths entwine
A tangled web for the fly designed

In disputed seas conflicts churn
As rival fires rise and burn

But the face of force has changed its guise
No longer bound to steel or ties

Soft words can shake as cannons roar
A culture's touch can shape the war

Corporations weave the threads of might
Beyond the flags, beyond the fight

So here we stand, the world unmade
By changing hands, by deals conveyed

To those who dream of peace's grace
Look not to strength, but to embrace

For notions and motions will twist and bend
Yet consciousness shapes how stories end.

Waging Veiled Wars

It's a different kind of oppression
Being trapped in your own wrecked tribulation
A prisoner of thoughts that hesitate
And a constant battle, as we suffocate

We know the source
Of our deepest pain
Yet struggle to find a way
To break the chain

We water wilted flowers
Nurturing them in vain
Then we feel sorrow deepen
And find, that the roots were slain

Castles of dreams
Built on shifting sands
Washed away by waves
Of restless hands

Each fragile fortress
Crumbling to dust
Leaves us with shards
Of shattered trust

We wage veiled wars
And tie our souls with string
The mind and heart wrestle
As if to witness, we bring

The weight of memories
The sting of the past
Threaten to drown us
In a cautionary cast

So we fight fervently
To find a firm voice
To calm the storms
And make a peaceful choice

To nurture strength
And let go of the pain
To rise above the waves
And *just breathe* again

Chained to Paint

Van Gogh swirls in oils of toil
Tempests caged within starry nights
His weary hands, his fevered mind
A sunlit dream he'll never find

Monet drowns in hues of the wind
Lilies blurred, dewed mornings singed
Fleeting perception he sought to portray
Still he painted a dissolving, muted decay

Picasso broke the delusions apart
Shards of faces, fractured art
What is whole? And what is real?
Ask the man who learned not to feel

Klimt's gold whined, fiending feel
Because gilded frames can't hold or seal
So beauty wilted, the colors prayed
A masterpiece, yet still afraid

Munch's scream still haunts me today
A soundless affliction, a vacant stare
Is this the fate of those who see?
To paint, to bleed, yet not be free?

Lost artists labored
Through brutal time
To echo through strokes
Only to remain benign

Still pressured, they tried
Their hearts black and blue
Visions left in endless rain
Turning stones, a depiction true

And so they drift, these spiritless souls
Wisps with wills and empty bowls
Starving minds in splendor's grave
Chained to the beauty that they crave.

Beam of Belief

Bleak, bitter,
Burnt or bare
This world will beat you
Blue for your wares

Like a stormy sea
It will crash and roar
But observe, it is simply
A barometer for your soul

Berate not, battle,
Burst nor break
Become instead
Bemuse and be brave

Don't bleed by its bricks, build and beware
Bathe in its beauty
Bloom, beam, and be fair
Behold a garden, in the warm sun's care

Do not belittle, blame, or abhor
Consult your brain
For goodness sake
Let understanding soar

Consider those
Who beweep and are bored
Bothered souls, with breaking backs are cored
Bearing burdens, browbeaten, and betrayed
Who brace, brush, and break free with grace

What beam do they bend?
Marvel, you may
Be baffled, boggled
Blink, I'll say
Persistent power, forever unbound
Their breath sustains with *belief* profound.

No Soul Weeps

No soul weeps for the phoenix's final breath
For she was forged in fire, destined to rise again

Yet beneath her wings of blazing light
She carries embers of scorching scars and fright

Those who gaze upward, mesmerized by her flight
Admire the brilliance, but to her defiance are blind

They almost expect her nest, to forever bloom
Unaware of the burn, beneath every plume

They see the spectacle of rebirth, the dazzling glow
But not the searing agony, of being consumed

She quietly screams, for wind and borage
They bring her the sun, wishing her old age

Masking tears that mingle, with molten stars
Fierce in emitting independence, she chars

Though every fiery trial, she settles hash
Her memories and self, are reduced to ash

A creature of paradox, both creation and casualty
She dreams of a pause, an unaffordable fantasy

Capturing beauty, in each soaring arc
Her descent into inferno, leaves a benchmark

Resilient, radiant, yet deeply wounded
Her rebirth is a cycle of exquisite torment

From reflection and solitude, soft fuel she forms
Exhausted by the pinches, of preparing to perform

So each time she transforms, putting up such a glorious
guise
Remember the costs, of such a spectacular rise

As you stand here in awe, by her show, amused
See how her wings carry hues of red, purple, bruised

Grieve the resting anguish, veiled by the splendor of her flight
For every spark had caught fire by her muted might

As every ascension was a ritual, flaunting demise
It wasn't beauty blazing, but her tireless poise.

Fault Lines

With feet under clay
In a precarious age
We walk on a turf whirling
At a dizzying pace

A gas-shrouded sphere
A celestial sway
A nuclear fireball
90 million miles away

Yet we deem this normal
This mundane strife
A skewed perspective
A myopic life

Our visions narrow
Our understanding poor
A collection of fleeting
Moments at the door

We toil, we struggle
In this earthly grind
Unaware of the vastness
Or our fundamental design

A whispered secret
Or a cosmic sigh
An acute reminder
That by simple breaths, we live and die

And so we catalogue borrowed time
Oblivious to the wilderness rhyme
With cautious steps and delicate dives
We scout abyssal depths where infinity lies

The universe spins, unheeding, wide,
While we chase meaning, side by side
Specks of dust in a cosmic design
We're asking for answers through fault lines.

I forgave you then. I forgive you now.

I stand at a battlefield of sentiments, torn in two
One fights with weary fists, for justice due
She craves integrity, raw, unsaid
Her battles feel endless, and hope seems dead

The other bends, with grace too pure
Forgiving easily, tender, unsure
A burden of peace, she carries still
Apologies whispered, against her will

Together they falter, a thread pulled tight
One clings to anger, one yields to midnight
Yet both forgive, though unseen, unheard
A gift unasked, no need for a word

Whose worth do I question, in the eyes of many?
Fighting battles with no soldiers, any
No cheers, no arms, to catch my fall
Only silent spectators, standing tall

To say "I'm sorry" is an easier task
Than the weight of sincerity they never ask
If easing their minds means that I will bend
Perhaps that's where the pain of breaking my bones will end

All I seek, is just one planted seed to know
The wounds I watered, the hurt I ploughed
That forgiveness doesn't mean that I am whole
But that understanding could throw some soil on my soul

In solace, faith becomes my shore
A trust in plans, the divine has in store
One who hears the burdens, that I cannot speak
And strengthens me, though I am weak

Yes, of course I smile, when hiding tears
Pinch my skin, to drown out these fears
Because I long to stand, unattended someday
Pleased without society, in every which way

Even when pain feels sharp and clear
Writing tempers every fear
Words strip the darkness from decreed despair
And place my burdens in celestial care

For I know no soul, bears more than it can hold
A truth I cling to, fierce and bold
Though hurt by one who turned away
I breathe and trust in brighter days

All I sought was space to be
For now you see, what pilots in me
You never *needed* to ask me how
I forgave you then. I forgive you now.

A Hidden Being

The vast species, a dynamic gene
Friendly souls or a villainous fiend

In hearty laughter or a wailing shriek
I observe a hidden being

Born with casts, both bright and faint
It shifts its colors, adapts, and acquaints

In youth, it wears vibrant shades
Dreams and hopes in bold parades

As it grows, its contrasts blend
Reflecting paths that twist and bend

In love's embrace, a fiery red
In loss, the blue of tears shed

Green of envy, gold of pride
Each emotion, a match to mind

Through trials fair, harsh and mild
It changes colors and reconciles

In every challenge, ordeal and stride
It is the chameleon that helps us bide

But beneath the layers, deep and true
Lies a being of constant hue

A core that stays despite the show
The essence of who we truly know.

Opine

An opinion is purely a view we hold
A judgment formed, but not foretold
A shortcut in the mind's quick race
To close the gap or fill a space

"I like to believe that there is a God"
A thought, a feeling, no façade
"Dinosaurs are cool," one might declare
How myths like "all are selfish" tear

Beware the line, "It's just my view"
For falsehoods may come cloaked in blue
Some thoughts are kind, while others sting
And words can wound, as sure as spring

Opinions grow from instincts bare
Born in the mind's swift need to care
They help us frame the world we see
But not all lead to clarity

Ask if all are equal, true?
Not when facts are misconstrued
Subjective thoughts of taste or tone
I'll concede are valid, if held as one's alone

Yet not all to opine deserve the light
When hate and harm step into sight
"You're free to think," the world may say
"But freedom's price in fact displays."

To say that one group holds no worth
Is falsehood forged in the darkest earth
Speech may be free, but consequence
Awaits the words that breed offense

In moments where, findings are thin
We start with what we have within
No time to wait for full insight
We act with what seems vaguely right

If faced with crisis or the new
Assumptions lead us, tried and true
Yet growth demands we pause, revise
To change what clouds our open skies

But suppose one faints or drops nearby
No ready manual to guide or try

Instinct may lead, then knowledge grows
Until reliability through action shows

Our minds are shaped by where we tread
By peer approval, or books we've read
Yet scrutiny must light the way
To test the thoughts that swerve or stay

Some beliefs may fade as trends arise
Yet fashion can be a veiled disguise
When they could prove just as obscene
Why trade old truths for newer lies?

Opinions guide us through the cream
They build the world where we can dream
But guard yourself from pride's quick hold
For none of us possess pure gold

Let change and knowledge be your guide
So thought can grow, and factuality abide
Believe me, learning can enable
For minds are meant to be malleable.

Between Delay and Dawn

Each dawn, I wake to see a fractured frame
This shattered glass, witness to the tick of time
Outside my window, I see it stay
Before the directors of duty call me away

There's a book on my desk, that lies open
Its pages whispering untold tales
Yearning for the gentle caress of my eyes
That seldom meet its written crux or wise

Beside me, an unfinished sweater awaits
Threads of thought suspended in half-light
Each stitch has been an ambition deferred
Moments meant for creation have been stolen as vision blurred

A heap of laundry rests upon my chair
And art, as yet unformed, lingers in the air
All but glimpses of endeavours postponed
Spirits caught in vows of "tomorrow" are in a chokehold

Entangled in strings of desire and delays
Tasks pile up like how unspoken obligations weigh
Each one growing more daunting despite
The number of knuckles and deadlines I bite

In the sanctuary of lists and idle planning
I find a comfort in procrastination, in thumbs twiddling
Even as few final moments approach
Their bitter taste of regrets have encroached

For every project that began with a spark
Now fades into apprehensions of inadequate charque
The excitement of creation curdling into compulsion
Potential was lost in the fog of hesitation

In the murk of indecision, I drift along
Caught in echoes of not yet, not quite and not at all
Where aspirations can drown or in sea be adrift
The promises of beginning remain graveyard shifts

Can we start as 12:01 ticks?
With trembling hands, avoiding piling bricks?
Choosing to break a cycle, though weary still
To overcome inertia, who writes a hefty bill

No longer shall I barter time for restless sleep
Tomorrow never granted unless embraced now outleap
In these small and uncertain steps
I reclaim contracts of changed doorsteps.

A Headache

An aura forms as a distant chime
A warning bell of pending time
A heavy pause, a weighted air
The mind entrapped in cautious care

Hours may crawl, or days may flee
Yet still, you wait in agony
An unseen guest, a rude dread
Storm clouds gathering overhead

It does not knock, no soft hello
But crashes in, a vicious blow
The head though brave, forgets fast
A tempest fierce, too wild not to blast

Each light a blade, each sound a spear
Each whisper roars too loud to bear
The world distorts, becomes unclear
A haze of ache draws ever near

No hail could beat with such disdain
No hammer strike with sharper pain
Its force not spread but half-ensnared
As if to mock the uninjured spare

To title it, would be a piece of cake
Would not suffice this serpentine's claim
Your temples throb, your eyes give way
To tributaries too deep to wipe away

No balm of hand, no tender stroke
Can lift the weight, or clear the smoke
Sleep, the traitor turns away
While vomit is your last airway

A pill, a rock to choke on down
Too weak to lift the tempest's crown
Water's bland, food's sword is sheath
The dying soldiers' last breath

To whom does one surrender now
With a storm that's already encircled the brow?
No foe to face, no truce to plead
Only orison stands, strong in need

Can't decide if it is cruel care
Or one of hell's own leeward lairs
But before this migraine, let plans remain
Because for plenty it is merely 'a headache'.

Ink Sublimes

Thought is through writing, this I have attested
Tracing the edges of buried diamonds I have tested
A diary pleads to stretch, trembling still
Afraid of the honesty its pages will spill

When I write, I start to see
The depths of my dubiety
Yet feeling is all I crave occasionally
No understanding or thoughts, to save in a gully

Some words make room for darker undertones
The questions rise, seeds of interest have been sown
Did they laugh with me, or just to show?
What realities lie hidden? Do I know?

Yet when I feel pain, I cannot ignore
The need to search for reasons more
To grasp and scratch to reveal its cause
Write it down, examine each wretched flaw

My friend's gaze, her distant tone,
The sense of being pushed alone
In that rejection, sharp and clear
Still, I write to quiet some fear

Faith whispers softly, as I try
Arranging letters as they dry
With every stroke, I ease the weight
Pain transformed by trust in fate

Though I long for comfort beyond this hand
I lean on the one who best of plans
Laden sacks of salt dissolve in real time
As though packaged ice by ink sublimes.

Burnt Pages

I burnt a novel of secret pages
Ashes rising, turning laments to ages
A wish to overcome the dark, to forget
Saw the flames mocked me with no regret

Halfway through, a Noor struck deep
Said some scars are etched too far to sweep
They heal, but never fade away
Reminders born of strain's ballet

I didn't want these scars, to chart my past
To haunt my dreams or hold me fast
Yet I kept a scrap, a burnt souvenir
Not for the pain, but for the fire, clear

Contradictions filled my every breath
I suffocate, though life's air's fresh
No wounds to see, but I still bleed
Where feelings cut, and sorrows feed

"Soldiers have bled from where no wounds were"
I read it once and felt the prowess of this literature
In battles fought within the mind
Where peace is fragile, hard to find

Blissful aesthetics of suffocation stay
Like air to lungs too tight for play
A hollow skull, drained and gray,
Melting toward breakdowns bay

I ask myself, "What's next? What now?
Who am I beneath this sore shroud?"
No answers come just empty space
A mirror showing a fading face

The sweat of being useless burns
As brilliant promise twists and turns
Perhaps toward an indifferent middle age
A tremendous triviality I contemplate

Yet still, I cling to this belief
That patience, too, may birth relief
Through squalls of qualm, I'll hold my ground
For ease must follow, if trouble I had found.

Choice and Chains

One day in class, we sat and heard
Of Hegel's grand, relentless word
A theory vast, a plan divine
Where all unfolds by a fated line

At first, I nodded, thought it true
That every soul, both old and new
Belonged within some predestined frame
A woven thread within a flame

But then he claimed oh, what disdain
That humankind was but a chain
A passive force, a silent steam
Drifting through some sculpted dream

A fire rose of a deep unrest
For history proves we have contest!
The wars we waged, the lines we drew
The moral codes we broke in two

Perhaps the start was not our hand
But did we kneel, or did we stand?
Did we not choose, with thought so grave
Who'd be the master, who the slave?

Who would breathe and who would starve?
Who'd have the right to read, to heal, to live in light?
Through revolution, blood, and pain,
Our hands have shaped the earth's refrain

And even now, in acts so small
The words you type, the names you call
The food you buy, the routes you tread
The books you ban, the thoughts you spread

Each ripple turns, each echo stays
No fate absolves the role we play
That gun you held was placed, it's true,
But did the trigger pull for you?

So do not tell me that we are still
That we are bound by unseen will
For though the tides may drag and pull
The choice was ours, we bore it full.

A Martyr's Tale

I was named after the first to fall
Let me tell you of a martyr's tale tall
Of a woman who, though frail and pale
Sumayyah bint Khayyat tipped the scale

From Habashah, she hailed with pride
In reverence, she stood, though torn and tried
A home in limbo, no tribe to claim
Neither free nor bound in name

When Makkah had roared with tribal might
Against the truth, against the light
Had sought to break, to shame, to kill
This woman had held her will

Bound and beaten, left to drain
Her zikr rose like falling rain
Not just a victim, not just a name
A woman stood, embraced the flame

Her courage lives, it whispers still
Even today when women rise, with iron wills
But oppression lingers, veiled, unseen
Woven deep in practice, mean

Not just a martyr, a mother, a wife
Warriors bright, who have seen strife
Not just victims, but veterans keen
In insurgent groups, on battle scenes

In the heart of nations, they built anew
From ashes rose a brighter view
Yet still they toil, unpaid, unseen
While cultures claim their worth obscene

From bodies torn to honor's rule
The blades that cut, the scars cruel
A silent sob, a world's despair
To note the woman, to truly care

Violence bruises both flesh and bones
From war-torn lands to home's patrol
In conflict's fire, they stand, they bleed
Yet hold the strength to lead, to heed

A seat at tables, can the future stand?
A superior chance that peace withstands?
Will this gift be forsworn?
Will their blood just run cold?

A world renewed must see them whole
Not just as victims, but in control
For every martyr, brave and strong
There stand a thousand, righting wrong.

www.ingramcontent.com/pod-product-compliance
Lightning Source LLC
LaVergne TN
LVHW010020200726
843495LV00015B/1843